Adventures of Zoey

The ABC's of AUTISM

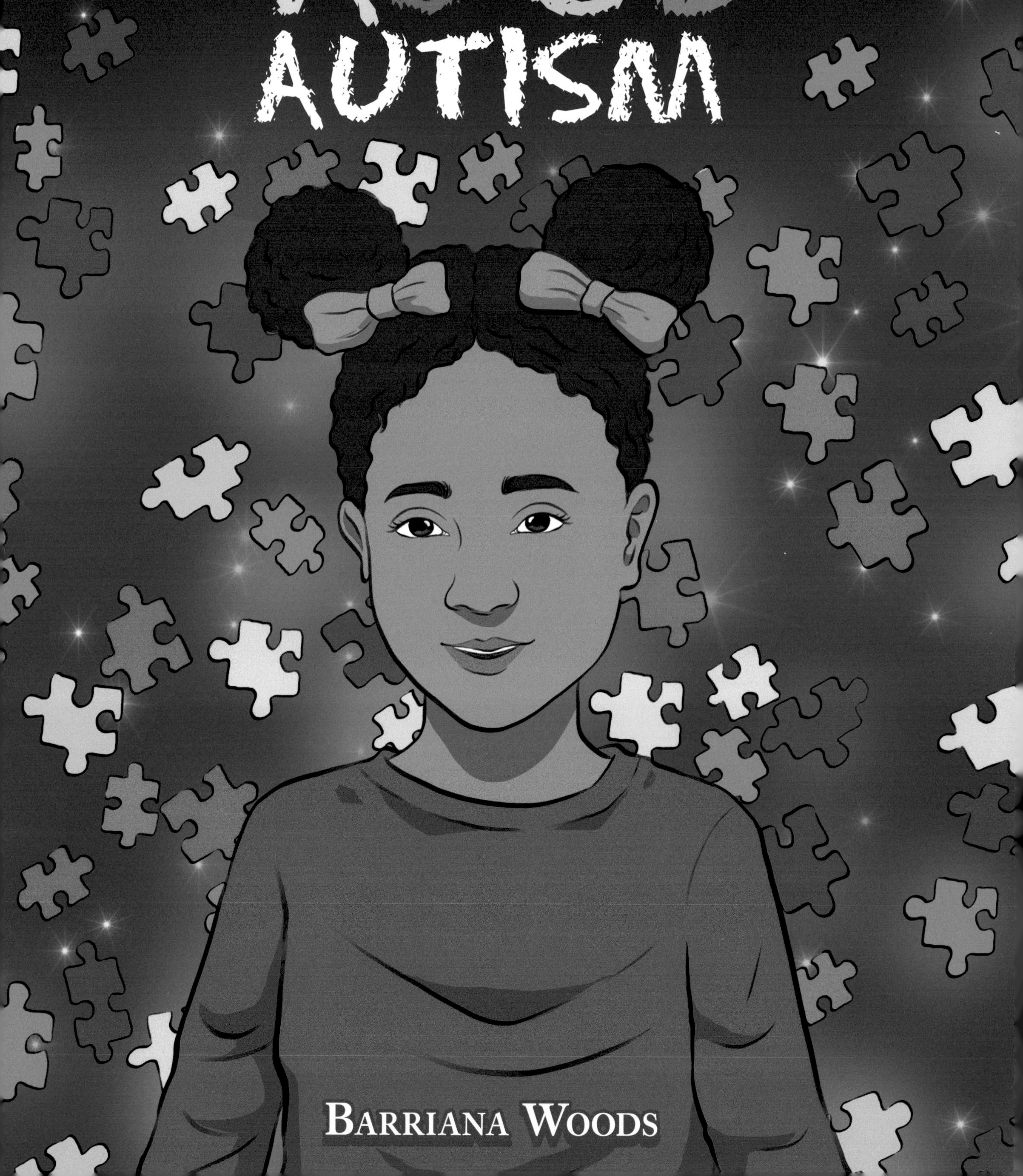

BARRIANA WOODS

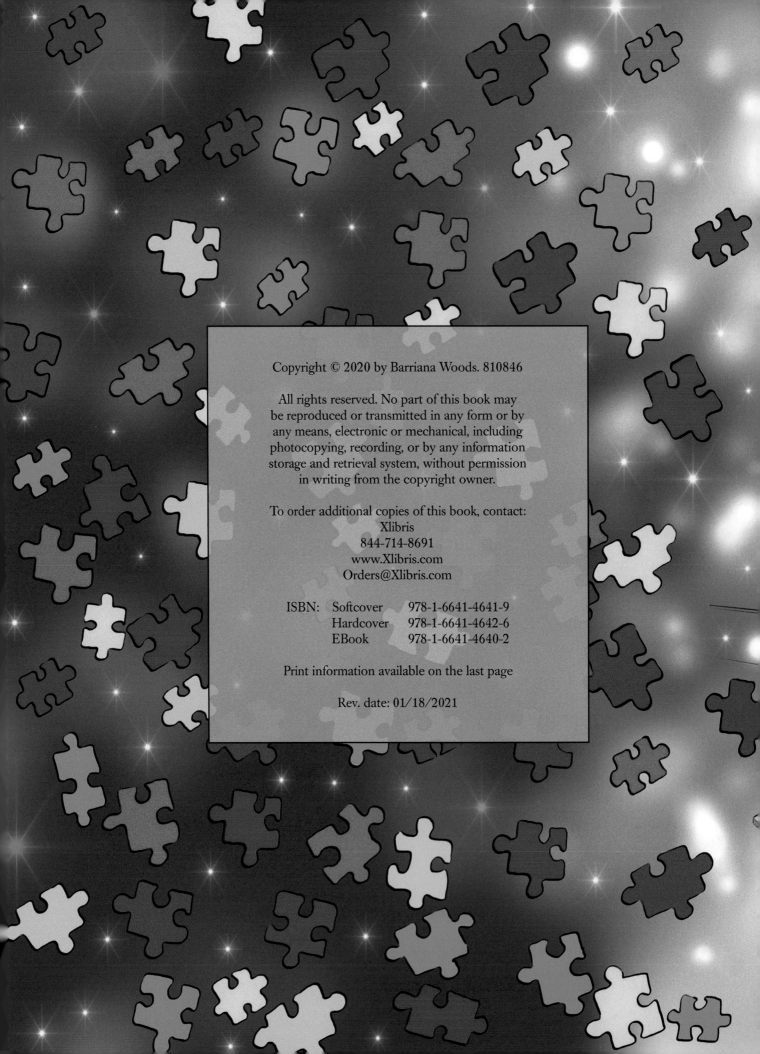

To order additional copies of this book, contact:
Xlibris
844-714-8691
www.Xlibris.com
Orders@Xlibris.com

ISBN: Softcover   978-1-6641-4641-9
        Hardcover   978-1-6641-4642-6
        EBook   978-1-6641-4640-2

Print information available on the last page

Rev. date: 01/18/2021

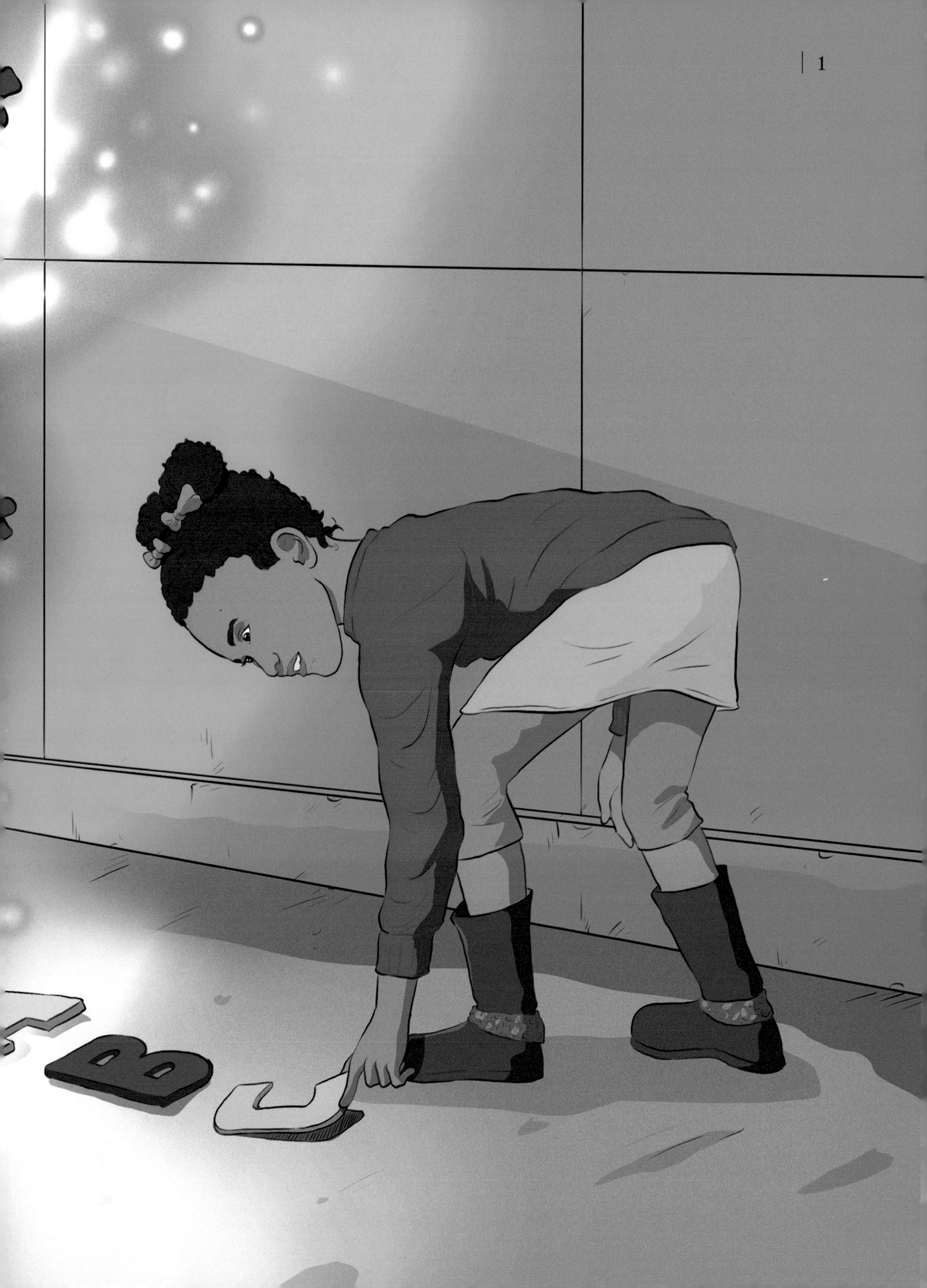

Hi my name is Zoey and I am on the Autism Spectrum. While autism does not look the same for everyone, I am here to tell you we all march to the beat of our own drum.

Now, I will tell you more about me. Starting with A and ending with Z.

is for **autism**, because it is a part of me.
I am **adventurous**, **active**, and **artsy**.

B is for **bouncing** and **babbling** with my **brother** because we are having fun. Even if I do not say it, I am thankful for our **bond**.

C is for **communication**, **creativity**, and **curiosity**. I am just like all the other kids you see. I use verbal and nonverbal ways to express how I feel and when I am **creating**, I like for it to be a big deal.

D is for **daring** to be **different**, *because all of us are.*
Even with my **diagnosis**, I am **destined** to go far.

E is for **echoing** others, while **exploring** how verbal language works and please know, I can still **empathize**, even if I do not look at you in your **eyes**.

F is for **family** and **friends** who love and accept me. I like **flapping** my hands because it makes me **feel free**.

is for **giggling**, **getting gifts**, and **going** on a bear hunt. When communicating, sometimes, I use **graphics** to tell people what I want.

H is for **hugs**, even if they are backwards. It does not take away from how much you make me **happy**.

I like **hopping**, **hula hooping**, and **hollering** too.
I also like shaking **hands** and saying "nice to meet you".

is for **imaginative** and **imitating** the things that I see, and at school, never letting an **IEP** define me.

J is for **jumping** up and down for **juice**, **jello**, or **jellybeans**. It is also for my sparkling new **jeans**.

K is for **kindness,** because it goes a long way, like a **kite** in the sky on a sunny day.

L is for **learning** at my own pace and **loving** you all, but also, needing my space.

I like **lining up** all the toys in a row and **laughing** out **loud**, as I spin out of control.

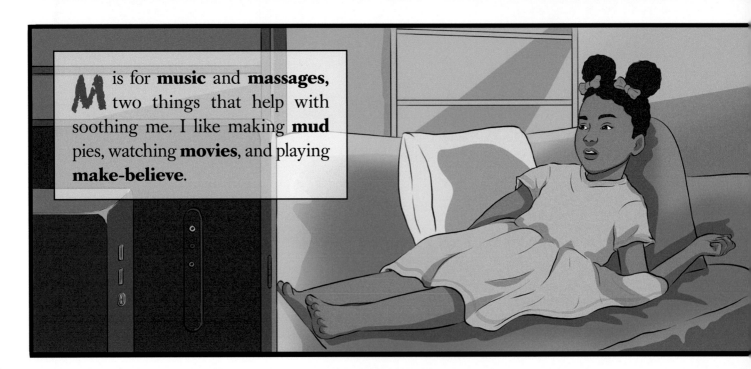

M is for **music** and **massages**, two things that help with soothing me. I like making **mud** pies, watching **movies**, and playing **make-believe**.

N is for **nervous** because *sometimes* the **noise** is too loud. I love **nature**, **nuggets**, and for my clothes to be **neat**; so, I lay a **napkin** on my skirt, whenever I eat.

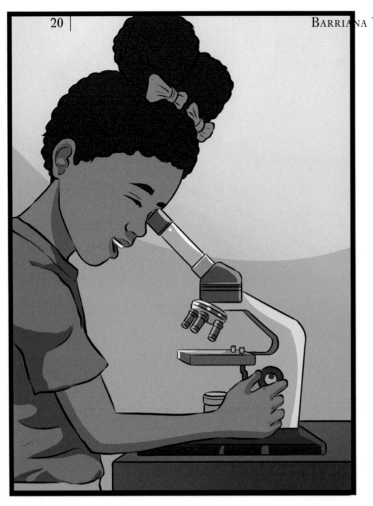

is for **observant**, **organized**, and **original**. Be **open** to learning about me as an individual. I really like for things to be in **order** and the things that I enjoy, I will do **over** and **over**.

Q is for **queen** because that is what I am. I learn **quickly** if it is something I am interested in. Even when things are hard, I know not to **quit**, just add it to my schedule and I will work on it.

R is for **running** or **relaxing**, there is really no in between, and not wanting anyone to change my everyday **routine**.

S is for **sensory overloads**, *sometimes* I need a break. If you see me **stimming**, I want you to know, everything is okay. What you hear and see, may not be the same for me, that is why at times, I randomly **scream**.

T is for **teachers** and **therapists** that care, I am always **thankful** for the **time** that they share.

U is for **understanding**, because that is what more people need to be. I am **unashamed** and **unafraid** because I like that I am **unique**.

is for **voice**, when and where I use it, is really my choice. When people hear me talk, they always rejoice.

W is for always **wanting** to have my way. I am **wild** about learning and having **water** for play. I really love the joy that it brings; however, I am not always **willing** to try new things.

X is for **Xylophone** and the sounds that it makes. I will achieve all my goals, no matter what it takes.

Let's GO !

Vamonos !

Y is for **YouTube**, if I could, I would be on it all day long. I like listening to all my favorite songs. In English, Spanish, French, or Japanese, I replay them until I **yawn** and fall asleep with ease.

Allons-y !

行こう!

Z is for Zoeybug, Zoey, Zozo, or just Zo, because all of these things describe me. I like **zebras**, **zombies**, and of course, the **zoo**, too. I can not wait to take more adventures with you.

Adventure Words:

Autism – A developmental disorder that impairs the ability to communicate and interact.

Diagnosis – The act of recognizing a disease from its signs and symptoms

IEP – A legal document under United States law that is developed for each public school child in the U.S. who needs special education.

Sensory overload – Occurs when one or more of the body's senses experiences over-stimulation from the environment.

Stimming – Behavior consisting of repetitive actions or movements

Printed in the United States
By Bookmasters